Maya Decides To Become A Vet

Dr. Keenya G. Mosley

Illustrator Sidra Maqbool

AuthorHouse™
1663 Liberty Drive
Bloomington, IN 47403
www.authorhouse.com
Phone: 833-262-8899

Because of the dynamic nature of the Internet, any web addresses or links contained in this book may have changed since publication and may no longer be valid. The views expressed in this work are solely those of the author and do not necessarily reflect the views of the publisher, and the publisher hereby disclaims any responsibility for them.

Any people depicted in stock imagery provided by Getty Images are models, and such images are being used for illustrative purposes only.
Certain stock imagery © Getty Images.

This book is printed on acid-free paper.

Front cover, back cover and interior image credit: Sidra Maqbool

ISBN: 979-8-8230-0584-5 (sc)
979-8-8230-0583-8 (e)

Library of Congress Control Number: 2023906653

Print information available on the last page.

Published by AuthorHouse 04/12/2023

author HOUSE®

Acknowledgement

Thank you to my mother, Sherrol A. Gray, and husband, Paul W. Mosley, Sr. for your unconditional love and support. To my sons, William and Paul II, thank you for always keeping me grounded. More importantly, to Maya, who has been a dream to watch, a joy to guide and a blessing to have as a daughter; thank you for being you.

I love you all!

Dedication

This book is dedicated to my late grandmothers, Jessie M. Jenkins & Annie Bolden Nance.

Jermaya was a quiet but curious little girl who enjoyed learning toys, stuffed animals, Barbie dolls, and *Dora the Explorer*. Her friends and family called her Maya. Her mornings began with going to Grandma Bolden's house before getting picked up for nursery school. Every morning Maya watched *Dora the Explorer* and learned something new. She especially enjoyed the monkey on the show. After each episode, she repeated the phrases that Dora introduced throughout the day.

Her inquiring mind was always tuned into conversations around her. She often listened carefully with a solemn look on her face. Maya enjoyed spending time with her brother William. Her mother, Keenya, overjoyed with having a daughter, desired for Maya to identify a talent by participating in different types of activities. She was quite a busy little girl.

Maya was fond of her stuffed animals, dolls, and the color purple. She spent hours playing with her teddy bears and dolls in her room with lavender-painted walls. Maya loved being around her toys in her bedroom during her free time. She especially enjoyed having family and friends over to share in time playing with her dolls and stuffed animals.

As a prekindergarten student, Maya was kind and often assisted the teacher. She took on leadership roles such as line leader, teacher assistant, and bathroom monitor. Outside of school, Maya was actively involved in cheerleading. She loved to attend practice and be around the older girls.

Maya took gymnastics classes, which helped her as a cheerleader. She held her head high as she walked along the balance beam. She wore a purple suede leotard and would swing around the bars with her trainer, who stood by to catch her if she fell.

Her mother often sat and watched very carefully. After every practice, Maya talked nonstop about how she performed. She was excited to try new stunts in gymnastics.

Maya was a quick learner. She would watch the behavior of others and mimic it. Her mother enrolled her into a finishing school, where she learned how to sit properly, hold her silverware, walk into a room and introduce herself, and talk on the telephone. Maya would practice these etiquette skills until they became a part of her normal routine.

Maya had participated in beauty pageants since she was six months old. In the beginning, she would smile or giggle when her mother tickled her during the pageants. When she became a toddler, she began formal training to walk on stage and pose. Maya did not want to continue with pageants, but she loved wearing pretty dresses, makeup on her face and being on stage.

Maya adored being on stage. She started participating in ballet, tap, and jazz when she was three years old. She enjoyed learning routines and performing them on stage. Maya was always excited to see the costumes the groups wore for recitals. Being on stage during recitals was very similar to performing in pageants. Maya's eyes lit up when she performed her routines.

Easter was a delightful time for Maya. She was able to use her memory skills. She rehearsed her speech every day for the Easter program. On Easter morning, she woke up with her new hairdo, and put on a frilly dress, ruffled socks, and shining shoes. She sat quietly occasionally looking in the audience to make sure her family was watching for her to say her speech. One of her favorite things to do during easter was to pet the bunny rabbits.

Maya played freely outdoors. Her time at the park with her brother William brought her a lot of joy. She often ran around, chasing behind him while going from the swings to slide to the monkey bars. She loved trips to the park, especially when she saw people in the park walking their dogs.

As a young girl, Maya was never afraid of dogs. She seemed to have a natural attraction for dogs and other animals, for that matter. When she and her family went to the local fair, they visited the animal section. It didn't smell very good, but Maya loved it. She seemed pleasantly curious to watch the animals. Visits to the fair would often lead to Maya talking about wanting a pet dog, but her parents politely refrained from the discussion.

One of Maya's fun childhood memories was attending a fall festival. She and her brother attended the event dressed up in their Halloween costumes. They enjoyed going from booth to booth for several hours. They played games and ate festival foods, like pizza and cotton candy. The last activity they did at the festival was ride a pony. Maya smiled from ear to ear while riding the pony in a circle. She talked about that pony ride for weeks afterwards.

13

Maya rode a school bus her first few years in school. She was so excited to join her brother in riding the big yellow school bus. The ride to school was sixty-three minutes long. She walked up the stairs and made her way to her seat every day of the week to sit with her brother on the school bus. Maya was proud to go to school; she went to bed every night excited about what the next day would bring. She loved learning new things.

If Maya wasn't playing with her brother or spending time with her family, she enjoyed educational games, especially those that challenged her. She sat for long periods of time learning new information through playing games. Her educational games were electronic games that grew in difficulty from phonics to reading and different levels of math.

Maya spent her summers attending camp. There she learned how to swim, make arts and crafts, and participate in athletic activities. Maya appreciated the freedom she had in the summer along with making new friends. Maya enjoyed the time she spent at summer camp.

Every summer, Maya went on vacation. She helped pack special items she wanted to take on the trip with her. Sometimes, she brought her Minnie Mouse purse or her Powerpuff Girls sneakers. Maya was particular about what she wore at a very early age. She was always excited about vacations that included visits to the zoo.

As a preadolescent, Maya was tall with caramel skin, long hair, and full lips. She often used her beautiful dark-brown eyes to carefully pay attention to the details around her. This was beneficial when she observed animals such as rabbits or birds. Sometimes she could be as quiet as a mouse, while other times she expressed herself with the use of her strong, raspy-sounding voice.

Maya became a part of a national organization that worked to improve the lives of children and their families. Every month she attended activities where she learned how to help others. She enjoyed helping others and took pride in learning new ways to assist her community to be a better place for everyone. Maya was learning how to become a leader.

With the arrival of Maya's baby brother, Paul, Maya immediately became a nurturing big sister. She held him and assisted with feedings as often as her parents allowed. As Paul grew older, Maya enjoyed teaching him new things. But most of all, she enjoyed the times she read her books to Paul.

As Maya grew older, she preferred reading books over any other activity. She had a lot of books on her bookshelf. She had different types of books, but the ones she loved the most included animals. She was super excited when she received the summer reading list. She could not wait to start reading prior to the first days of school.

Maya made high honor roll, cheered, and took ballet. Yet, she had to make an unexpected change in her life. Her brother had graduated from eighth grade and was about to attend high school.

Maya's parents wanted to keep them together at the same school and decided to move them to a new school. Maya wasn't bothered, as she liked being in school with her older brother.

Maya treasured attending school with her oldest brother, William. She talked to him every day about her teachers, friends, and desire to have a pet dog. She adored being his little sister and being under his care when she was away from home.

Maya prepared for her new school with summer readings, new uniforms, and a buddy. She spent her summer going through each book and carefully understanding the content from each page. She maintained a stern look on her face as she finished the books one by one and was anxious to start the next one. With each book, she kept a log. Maya was proud of her preparation for fourth grade.

Maya began attending her new school with her brother, where they were now car riders. She sat eagerly in the car every day on the ride to school. She always prepared to participate in class by reading and doing homework the night before. Maya took pride in being a good student. She enjoyed receiving her graded papers back from her teachers. She tried to anticipate how well she did before seeing her grades.

Maya was accustomed to wearing uniforms; she had worn them since entering first grade. She was particular about her socks and hairbows, as she could show her unique style through them. After meeting her new school buddy, she began to feel somewhat connected to her new school home, but there was one thing that stood out the most about her new school.

Maya was very interested in her new science class. There were pieces of lab equipment and animals everywhere she looked. She was amazed when the teacher announced students could take the animals home over the weekend. Maya overwhelmed with excitement told her parents she wanted to bring one of the animals home. Maya brought a guinea pig home and cared for it the entire weekend. When she arrived home from school on Monday, after returning the guinea pig to her fourth-grade teacher, Maya decided she would become a veterinarian.

About the Author

Dr. Keenya G. Mosley was born and raised in Savannah, Georgia. She received a Bachelor of Science degree from Alabama State University, a Master of Education degree from Columbia College and a Ph.D. from Jackson State University. She is an educator with over 25 years of educational experience. Her experience in education spans across levels from early childhood to post-secondary. She has taught, mentored, and advised students in pursuit of an undergraduate degree while assisting them in chartering their career paths. Some of her career experiences include teaching, strategic planning, faculty development, college recruitment, retention, assessment, accreditation, marketing, and career preparation. In addition, Dr. Mosley is a servant leader holding leadership positions in multiple organizations. She is a philanthropist and serial entrepreneur. However, her most important job is being a mother. As a mother, Dr. Mosley supports her children's efforts to pursue their dreams. Her son, William obtained a degree in architecture while her youngest son Paul, is pursuing a degree in computer animation and her daughter, Maya is a veterinarian. In her spare time, Dr. Mosley enjoys traveling with her husband, Paul Sr.

Printed in the United States
by Baker & Taylor Publisher Services